Finding Alaska Again

Artistic Images of Aquatic Creatures...
to Color!

Brittney Kauffman

First Printing, 2015

ISBN 0692515119

Inkedfoxbybrittney.com
www.facebook.com/artbybrittneyk
inkedfoxak@gmail.com

Guidelines

1. Gently tear or cut the page of your choosing out of the coloring book.
2. Color your page using colored pencils, fine-tip markers, or fine-tip pens. It's your art, so these are just suggestions. (I personally use Staedtler marker pens)
3. Find the word 'Alaska' hidden in your drawing.
4. Display! Each page is 8x10 and one-sided for the purpose of being able to display your work. (8x10 is also a standard frame size)

Most of all, have fun!

Can't find 'Alaska' in your drawing? Look to the back of the book for help!

Dedicated to my family, friends, and fans who have supported me and my art.
Cover photo colored by Laurie Kirby

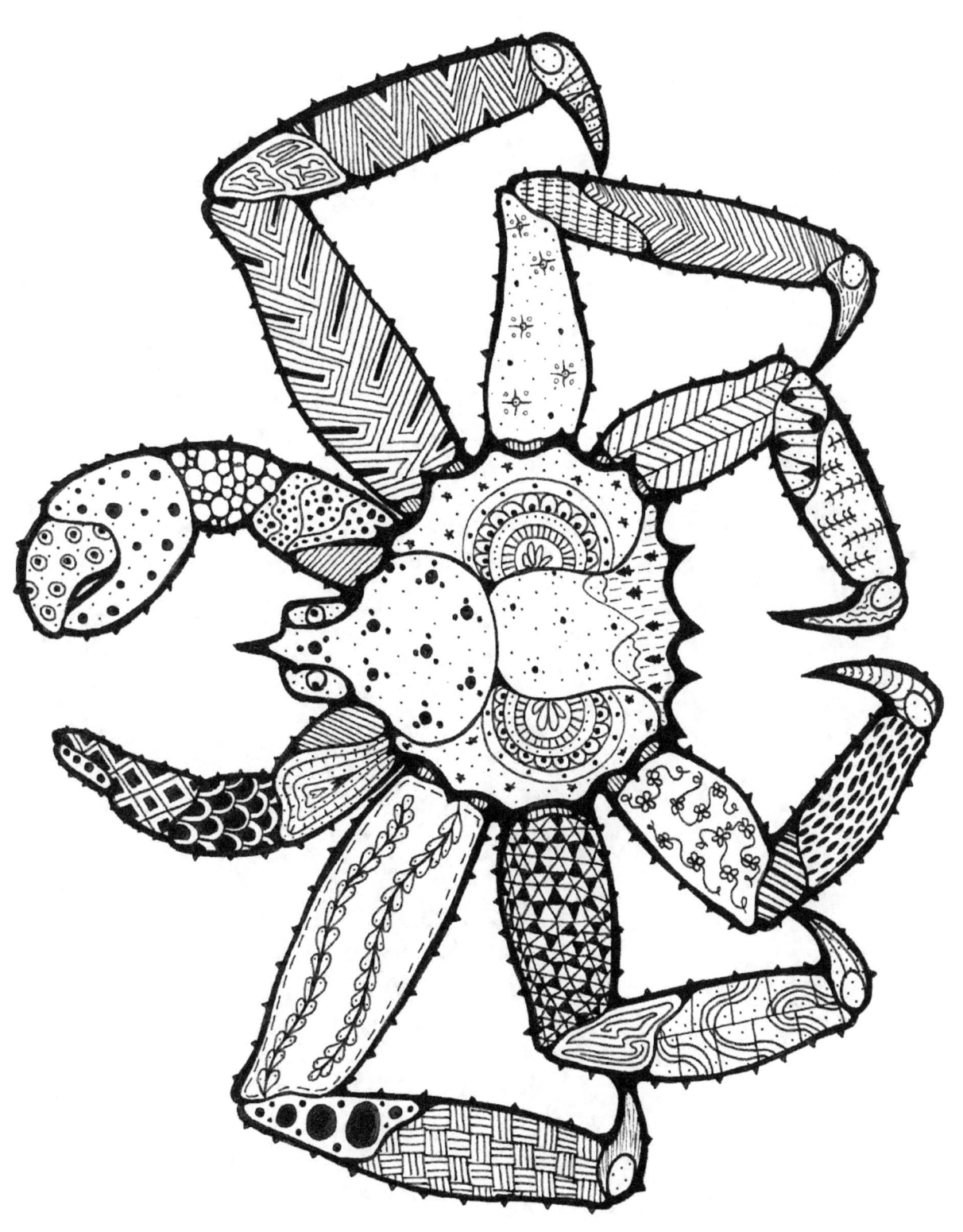

Red King Crab

Fun Fact: Males can weigh up to 24 pounds
with a 5 foot leg span

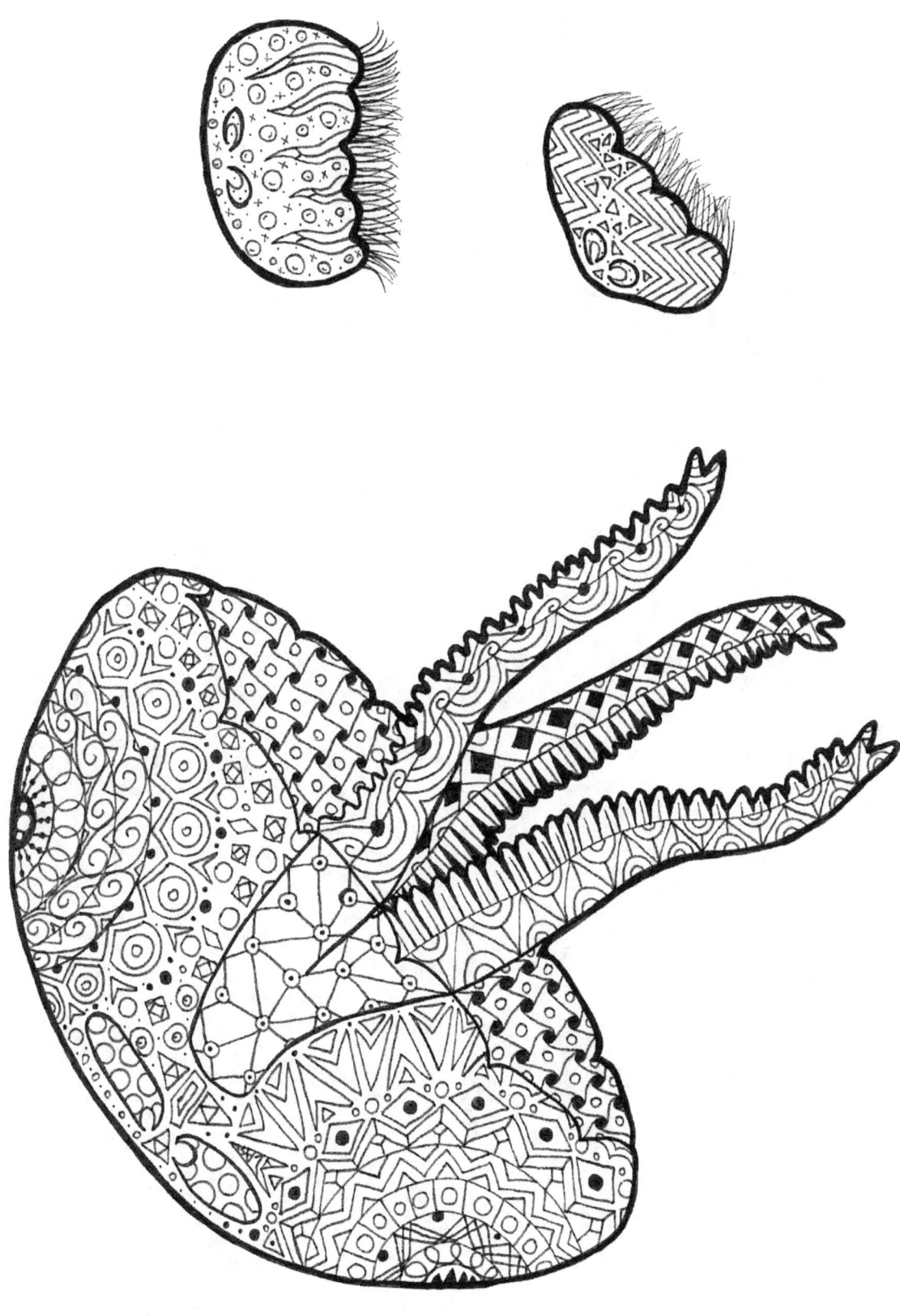

Jellyfish

Fun Fact: In the 1990's the jellyfish population in the Bering Sea increased drastically, causing many problems for fishermen.

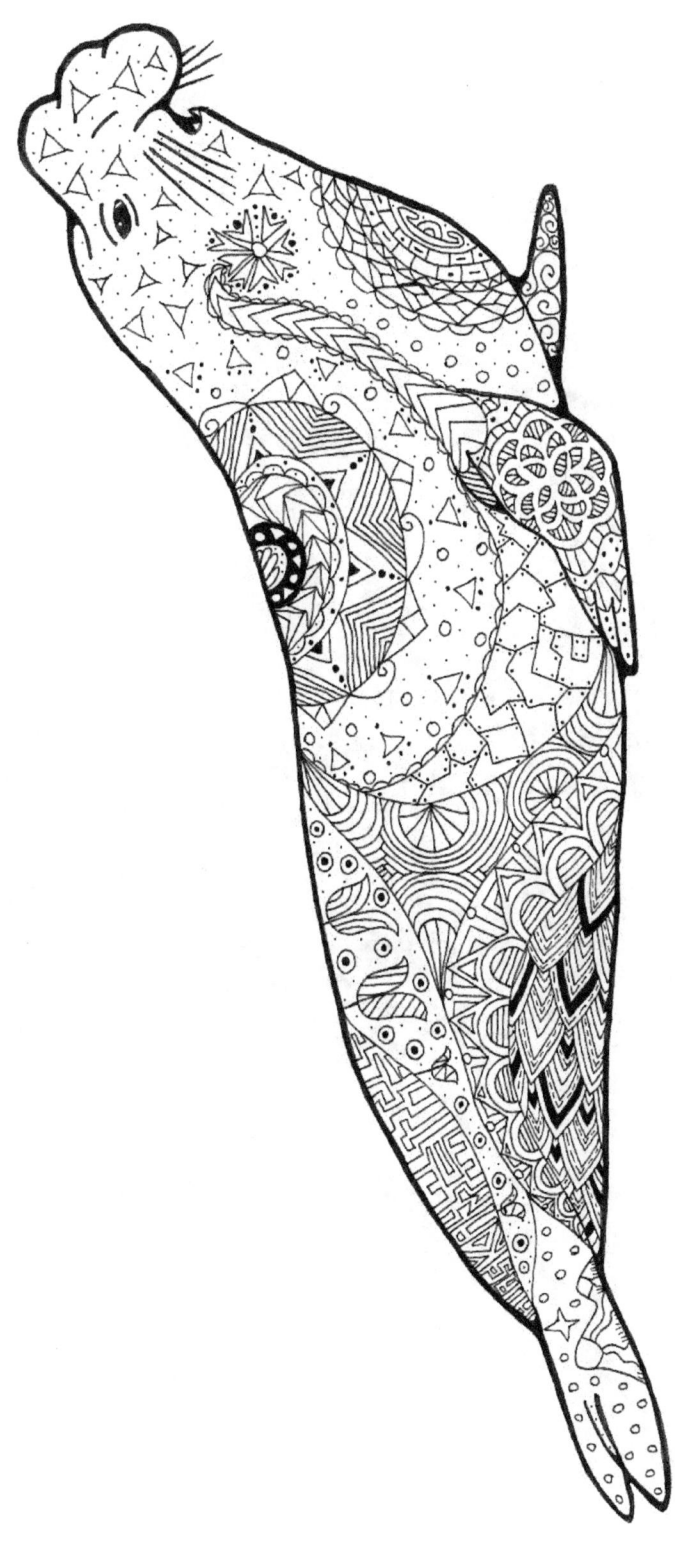

Elephant Seal

Fun Fact: This mammal's big nose is called a 'proboscis'. Elephant seals migrate from Mexico and California for breeding to Alaska for feeding, and back to Mexico or California, all in one year!

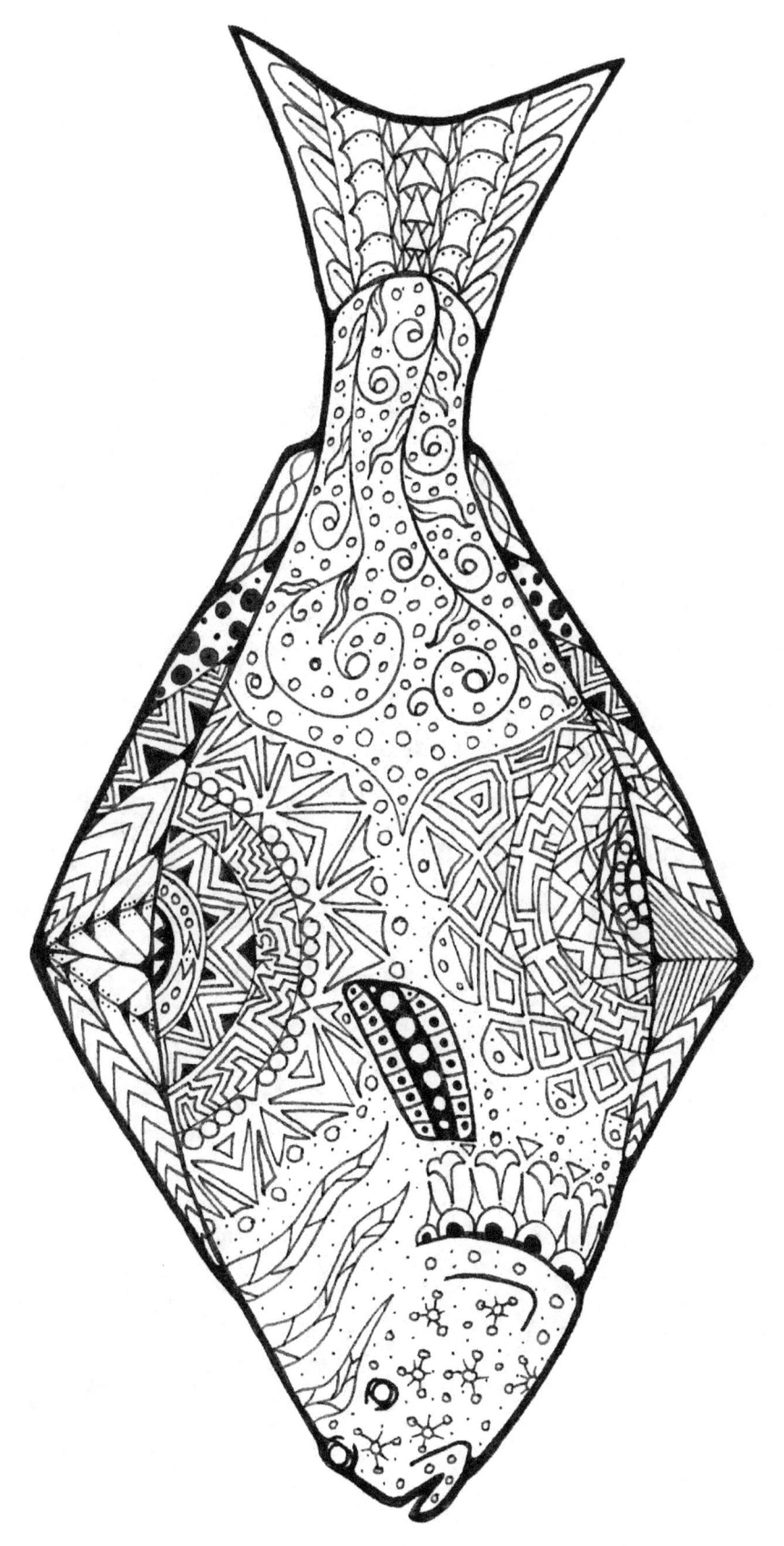

Halibut

Fun Fact: Large halibut are called 'barn doors' while small halibut are called 'chickens.' These fish begin upright with an eyeball on either side, the left eye travels to the opposite side as it grows.

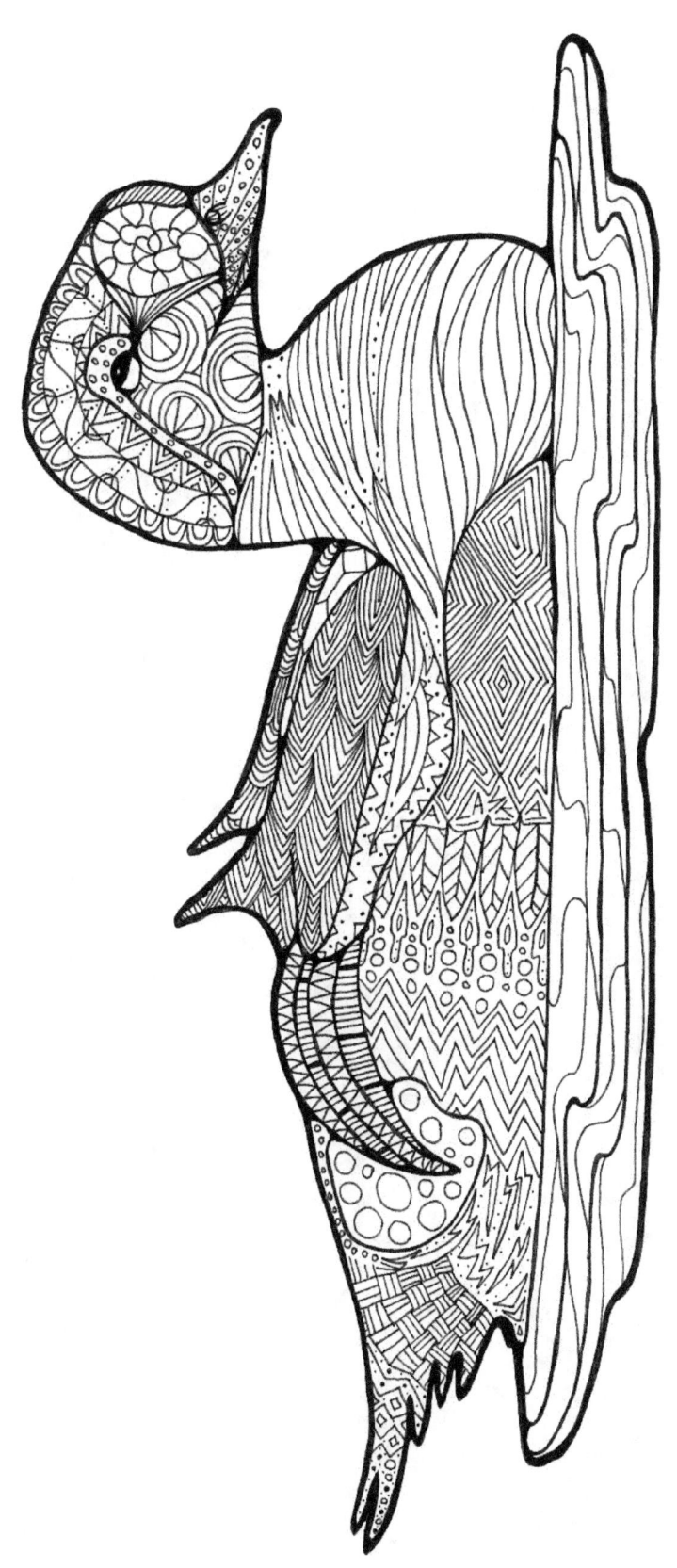

King Eider

Fun Fact: Most of these ducks spend the winter in the Alaska islands and peninsula.

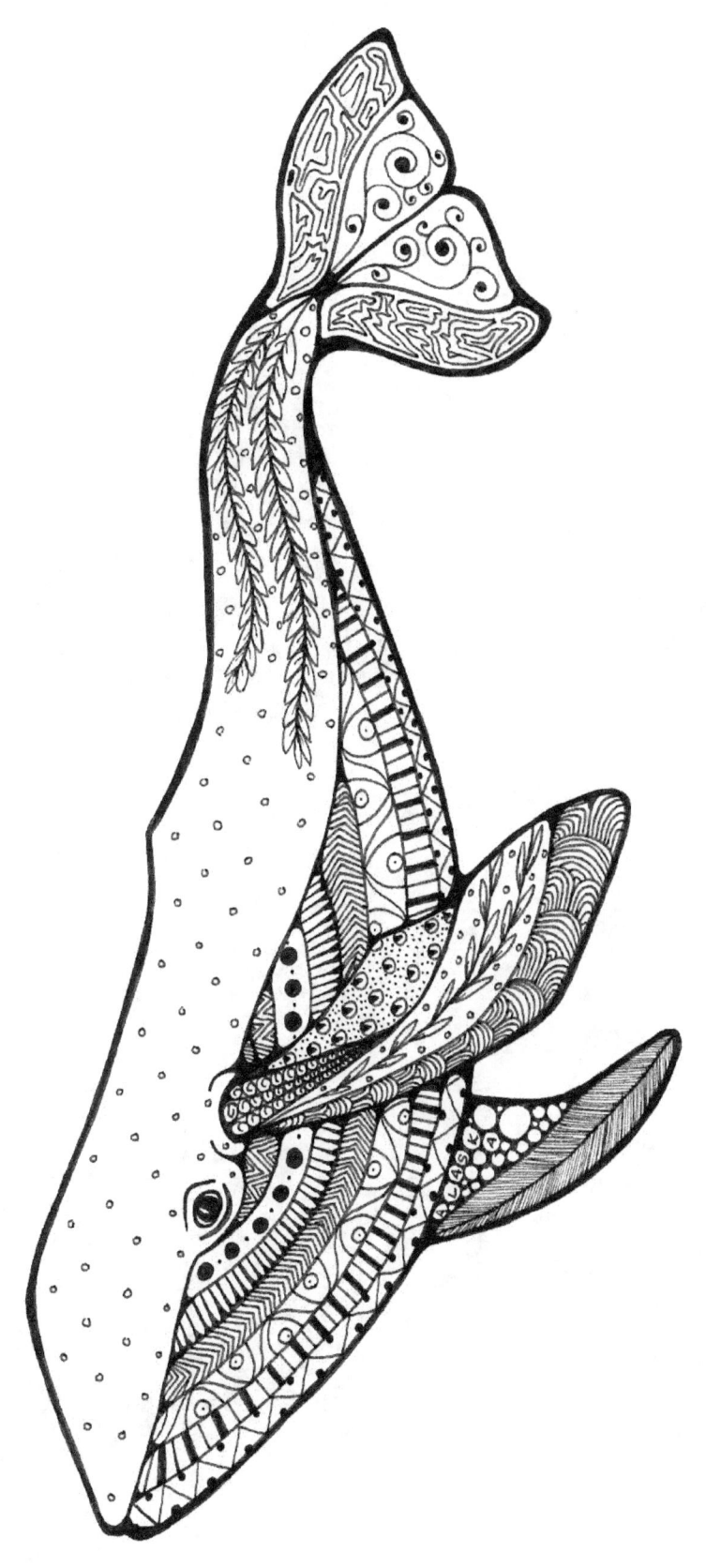

Humpback Whale

Fun Fact: These whales are listed as endangered. Their lifespan is 40-50 years.

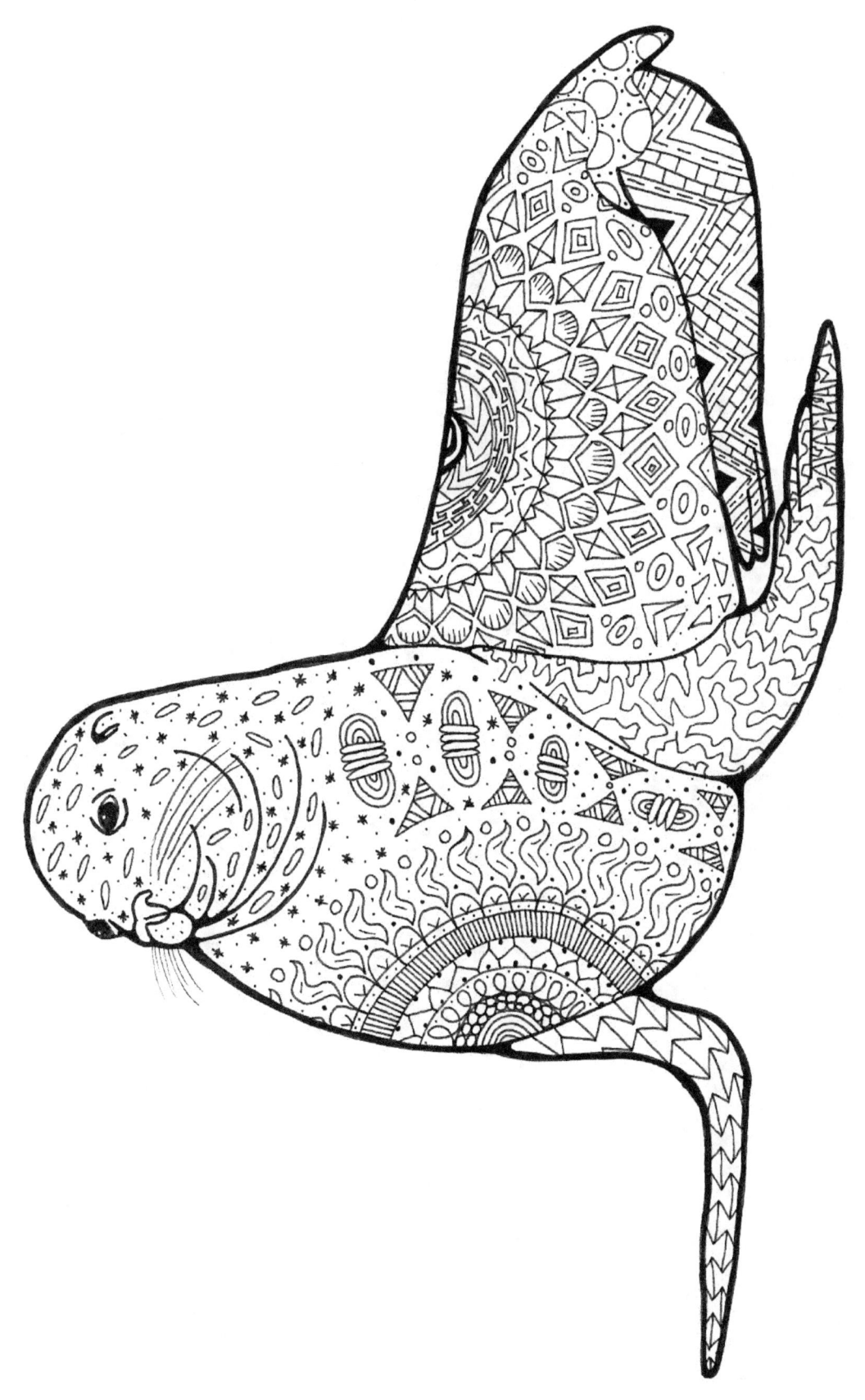

Steller Sea Lion

Fun Fact: These are the largest of the eared seals. Males grow to be twice the size of the females.

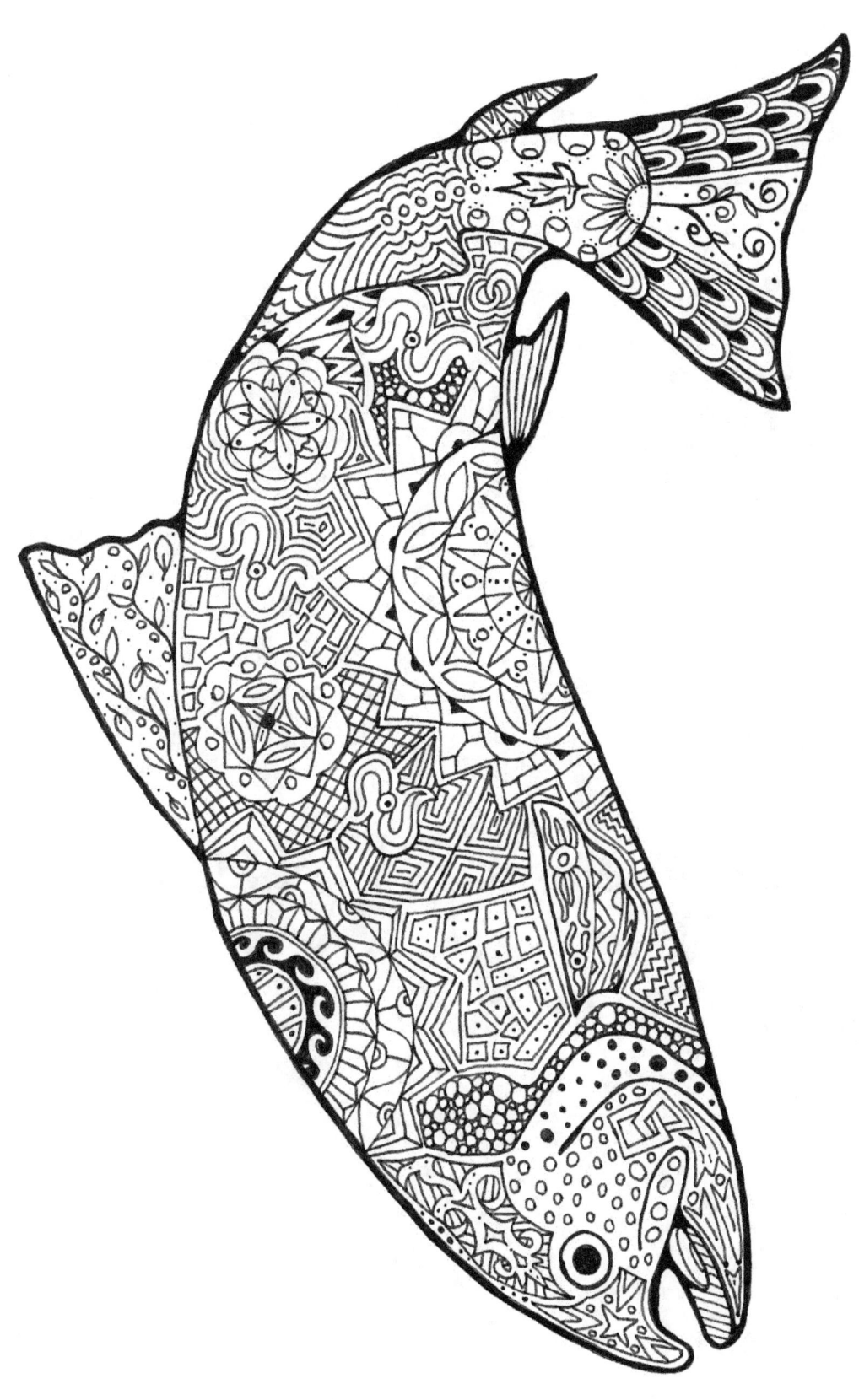

Pink Salmon

Fun Fact: A pink salmon goes through its entire life cycle in just 2 years!
They migrate immediately to the ocean and typically do not eat at all on
their way.

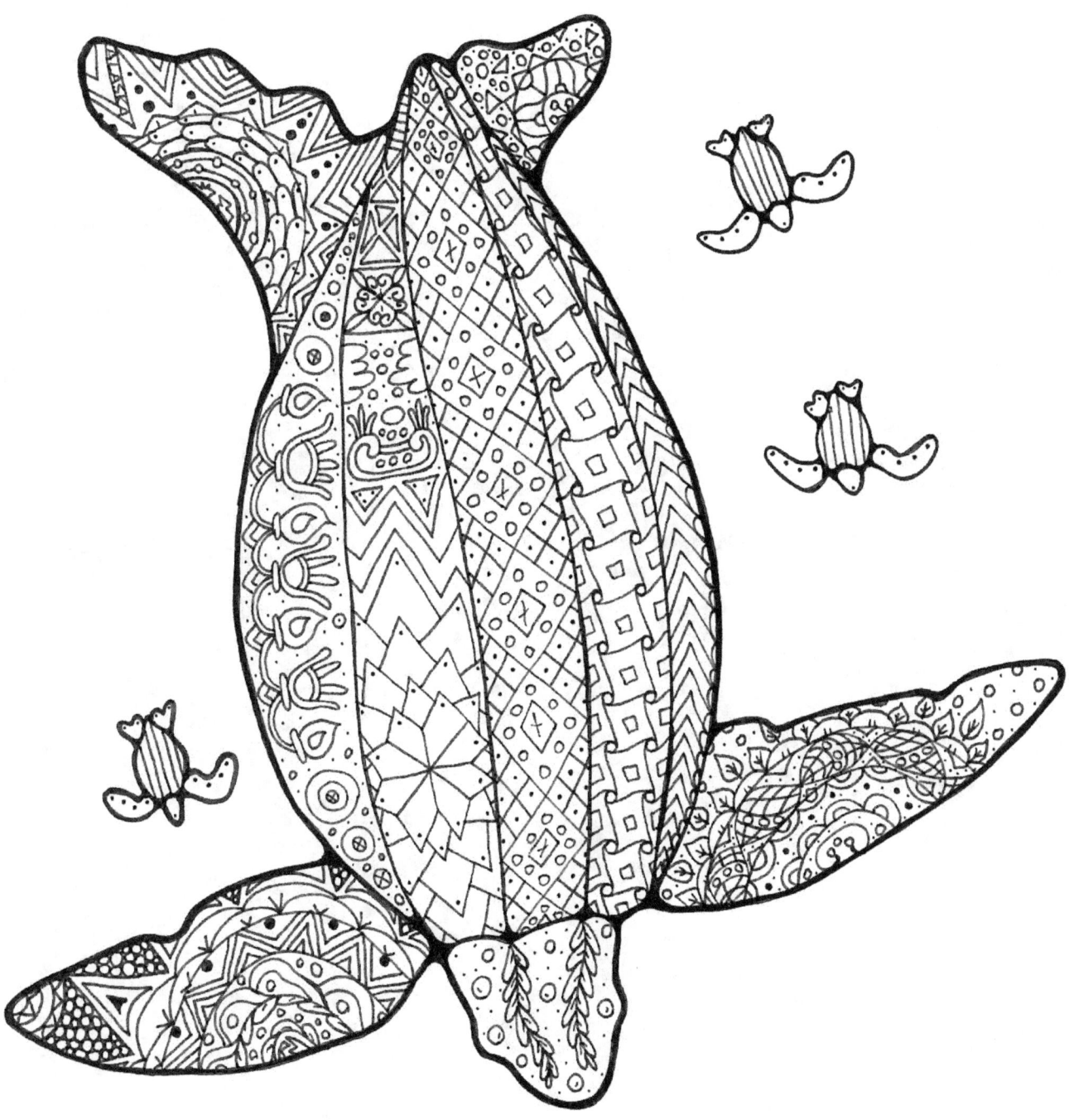

Leatherback Sea Turtle

Fun Fact: This is the largest turtle, and the most migratory, moving nearly 7000 miles in a year from nesting to foraging areas. Unlike most sea turtles, this one has a soft-shelled back.

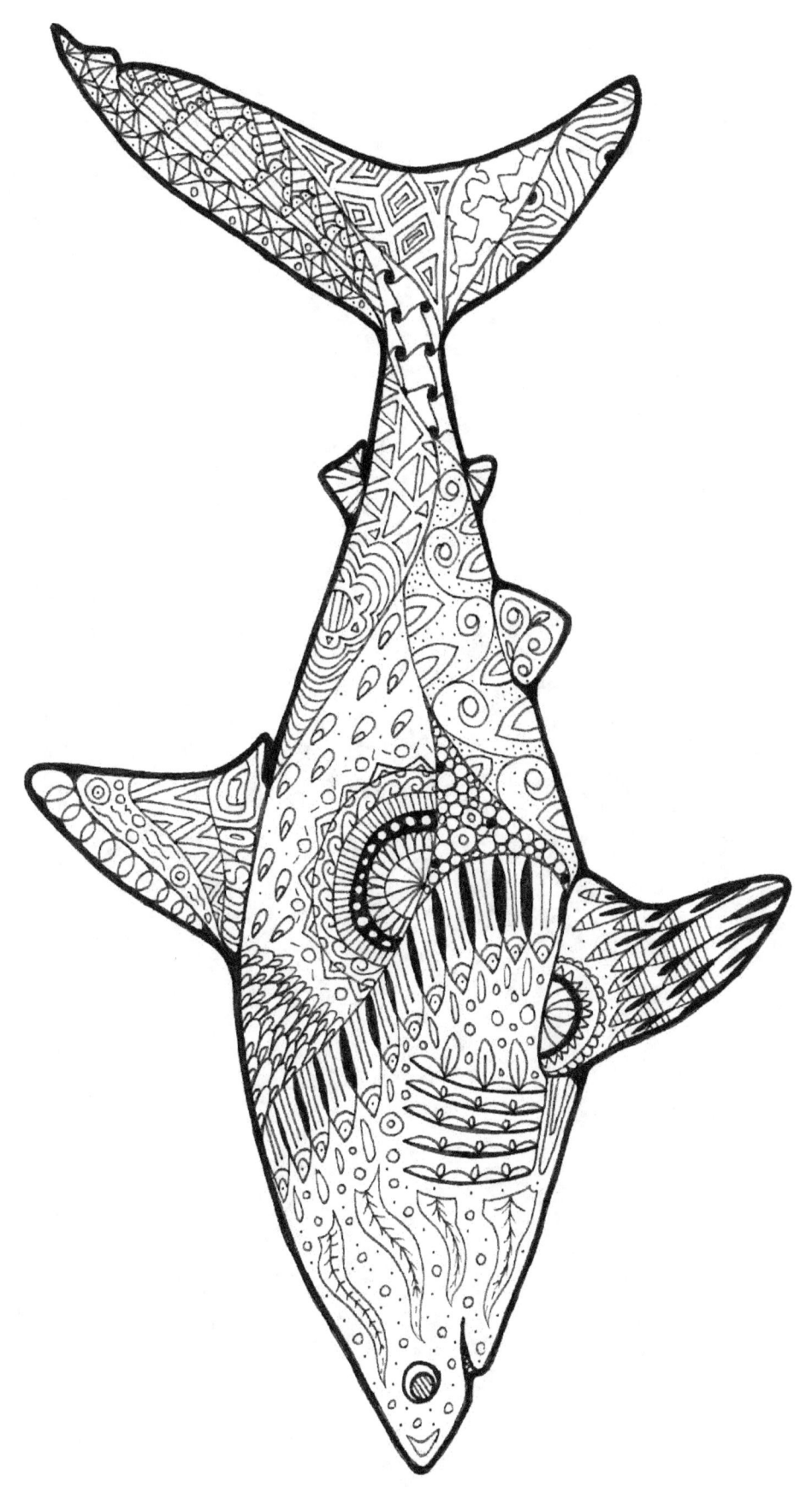

Salmon Shark

Fun Fact: On average they are 6-8 feet in length. Their offspring are known as 'pups.'

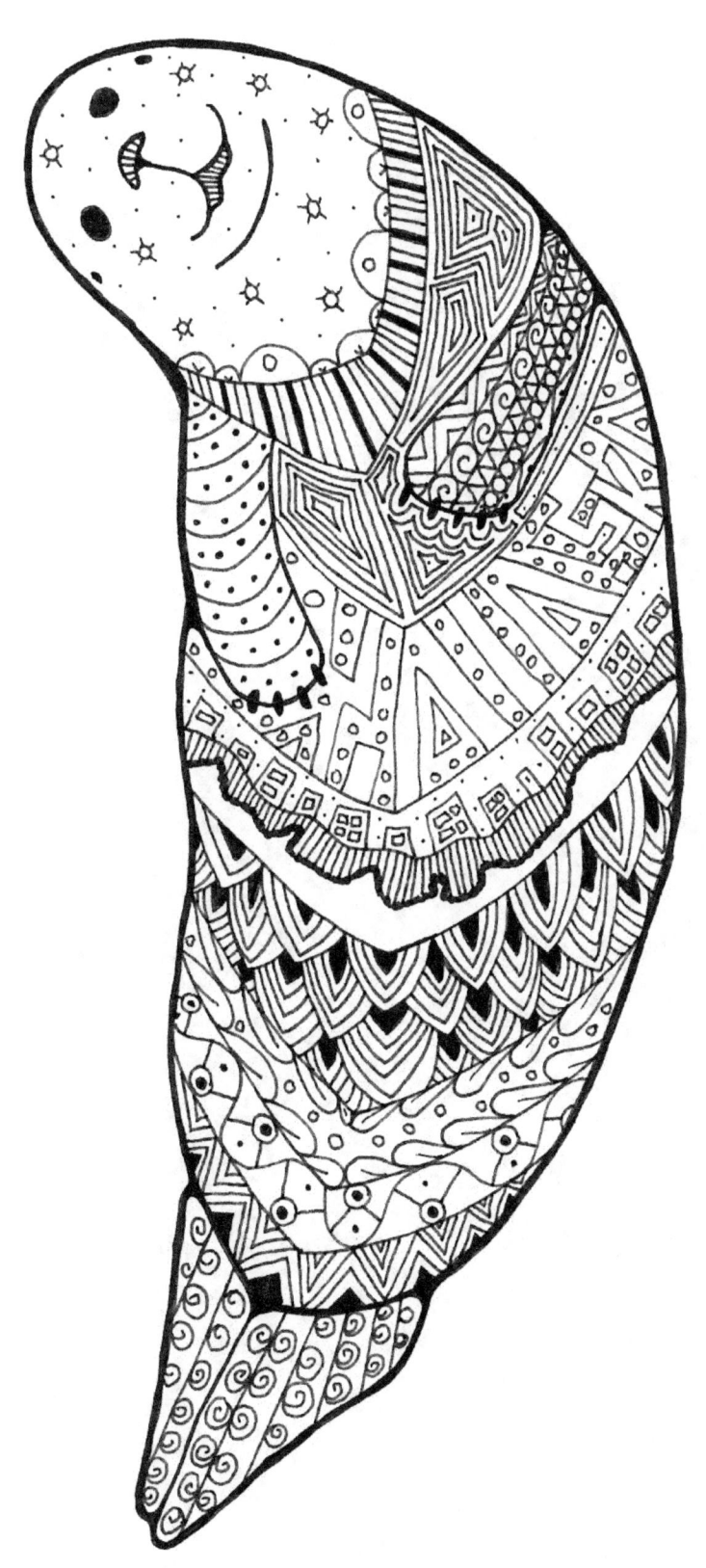

Harbor Seal

Fun Fact: They can dive over 1600 feet and are able to stay under water for over 20 minutes.

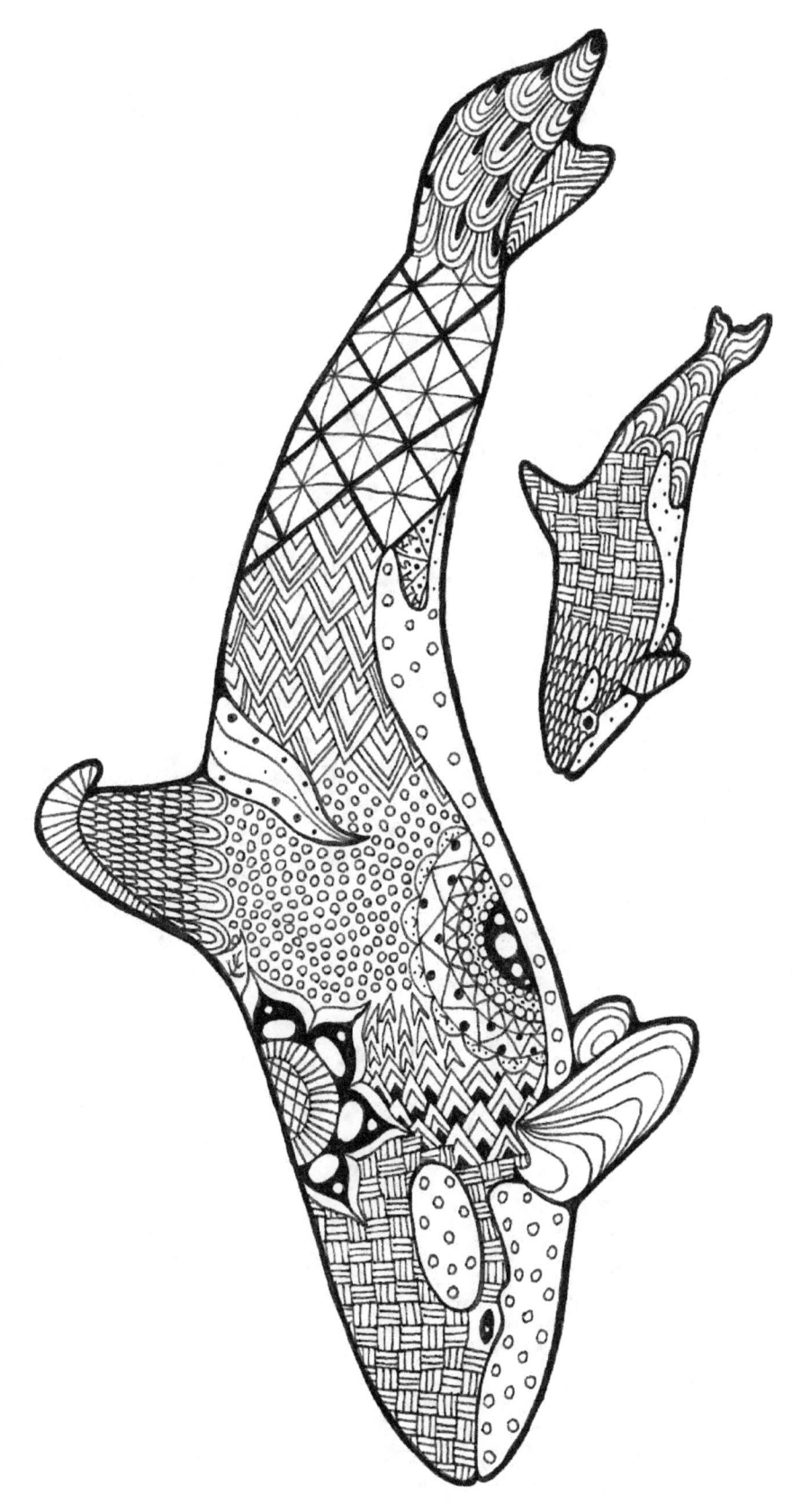

Orca (Killer Whale)

Fun Fact: These whales can beach themselves to grab large marine mammals off the beach.

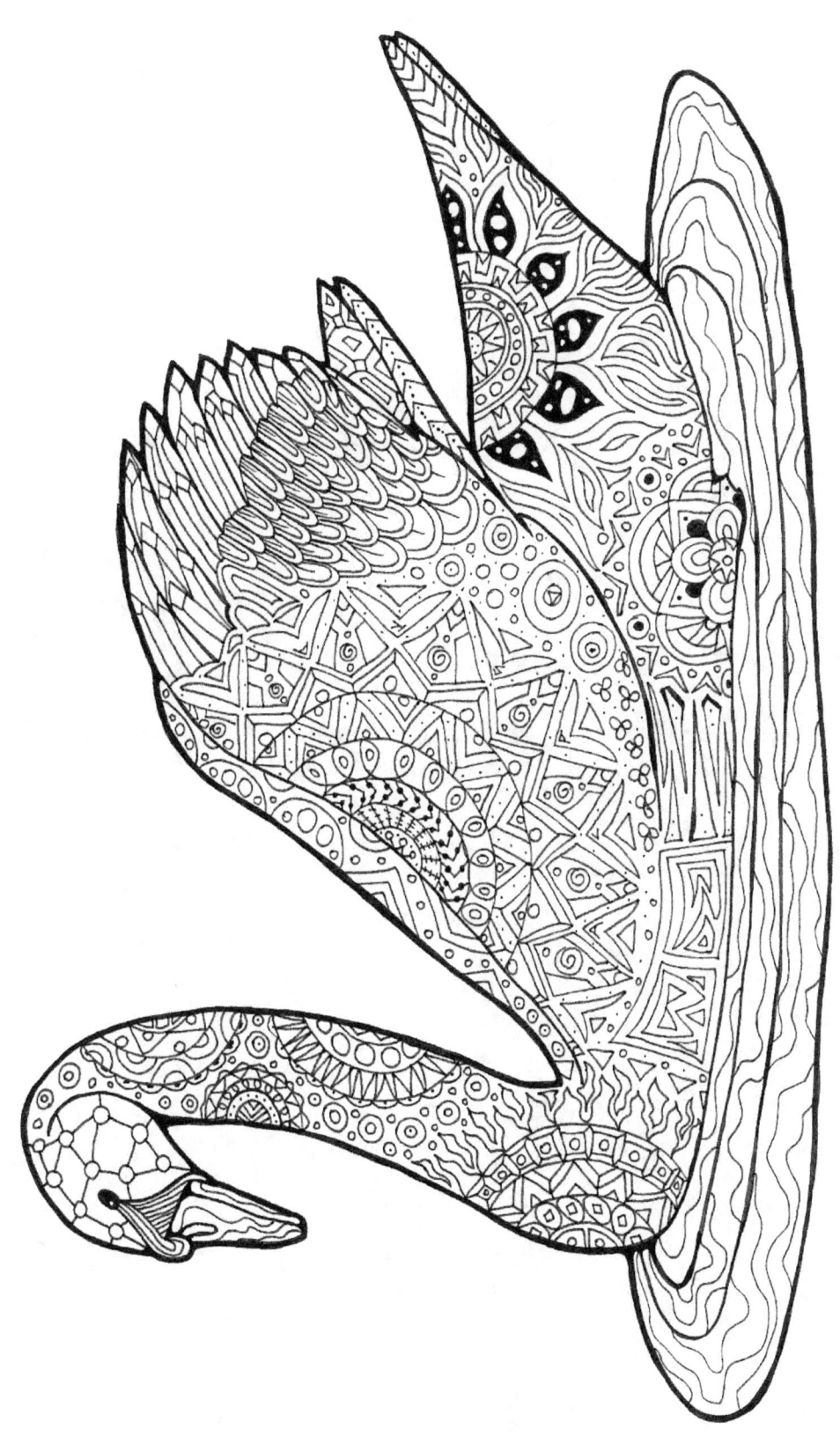

Trumpeter Swan

Fun Fact: Trumpeter swans mate for life around 2 years of age. The female trumpeter swan is called a 'pen' and her mate is called the 'cob.'

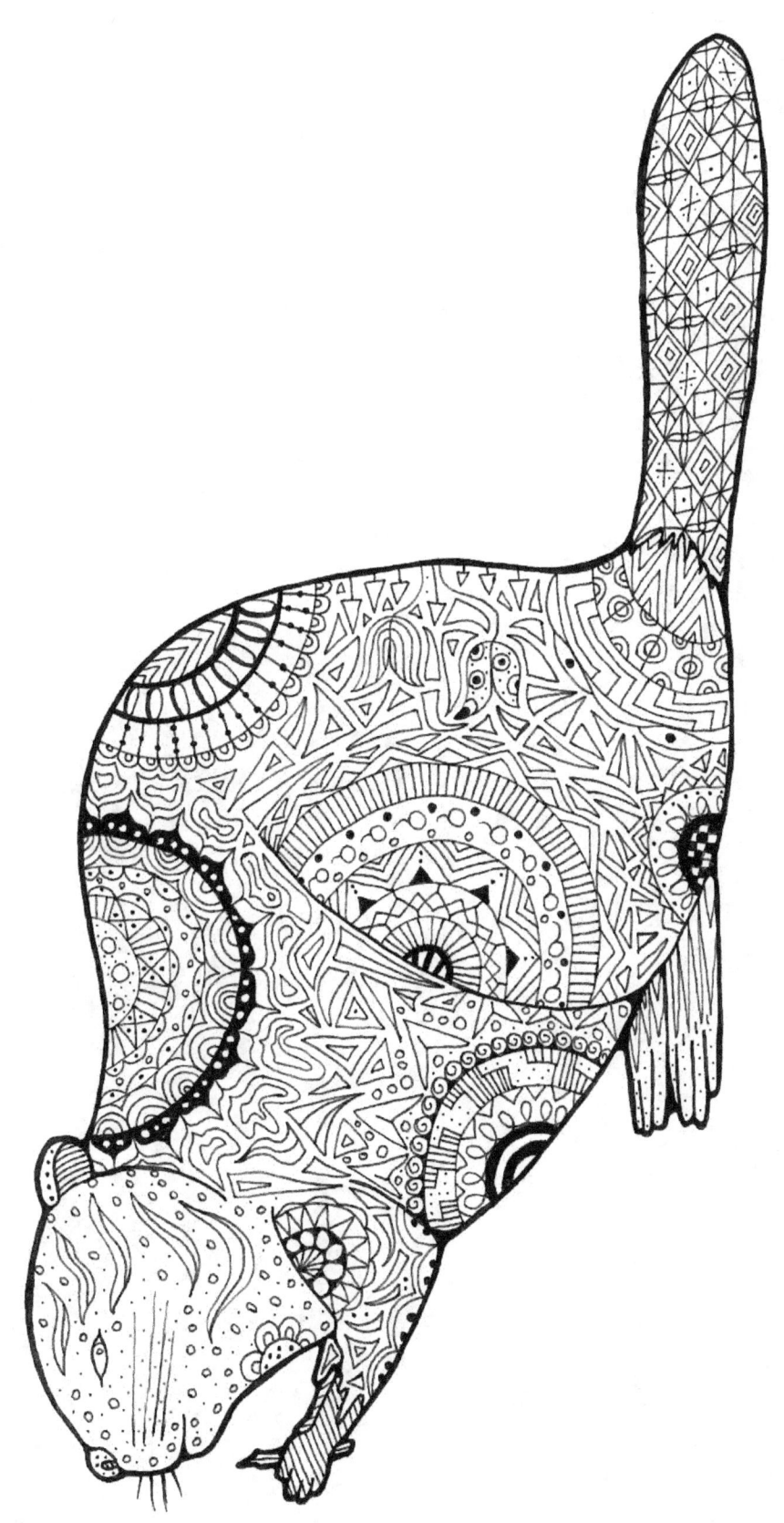

Beaver

Fun Fact: This is the largest rodent in North America, and it was introduced to Kodiak Island in 1925.

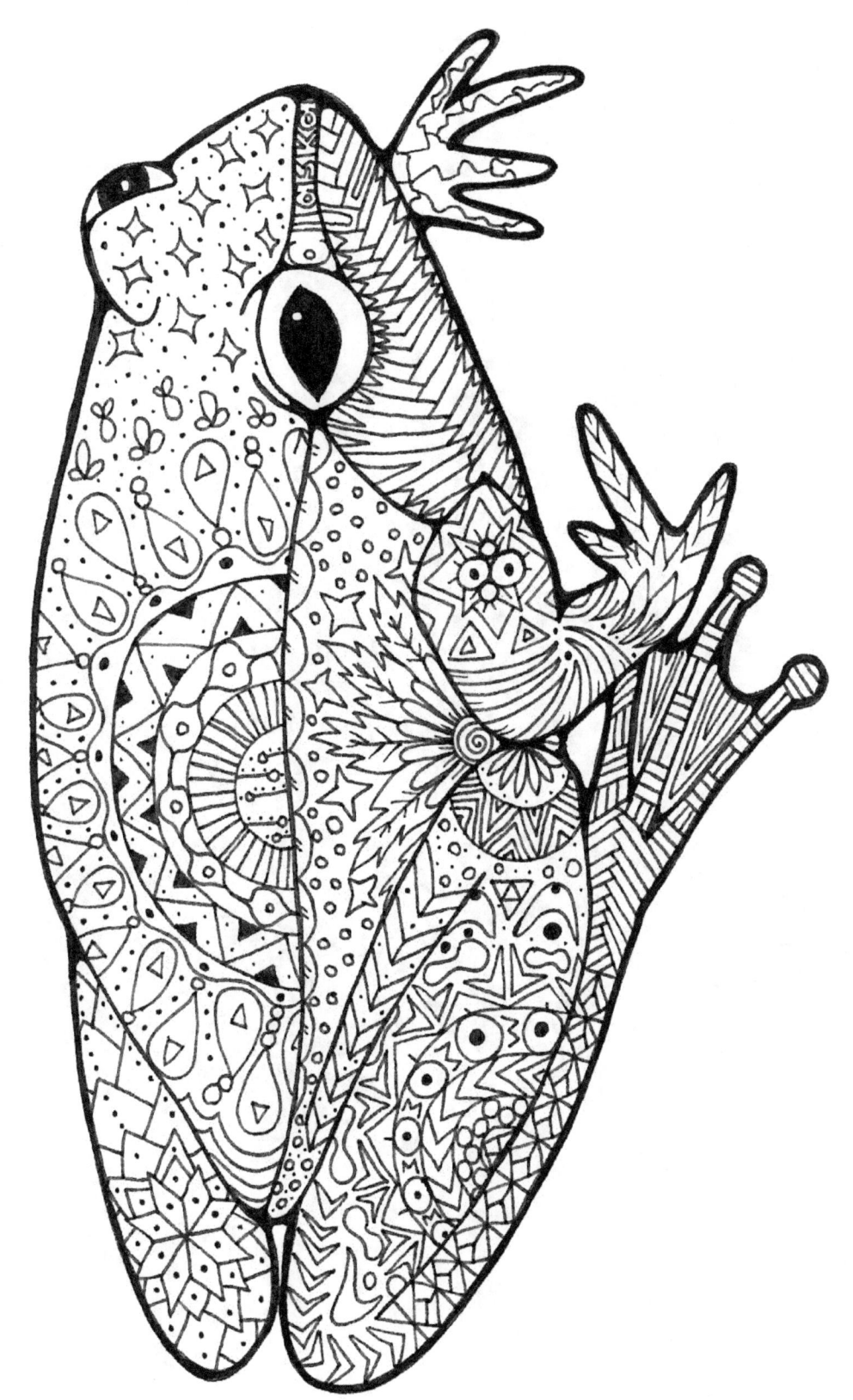

Wood Frog

Fun Fact: During the winter months, they can freeze and thaw 2/3 of their body's water for days or weeks at a time.

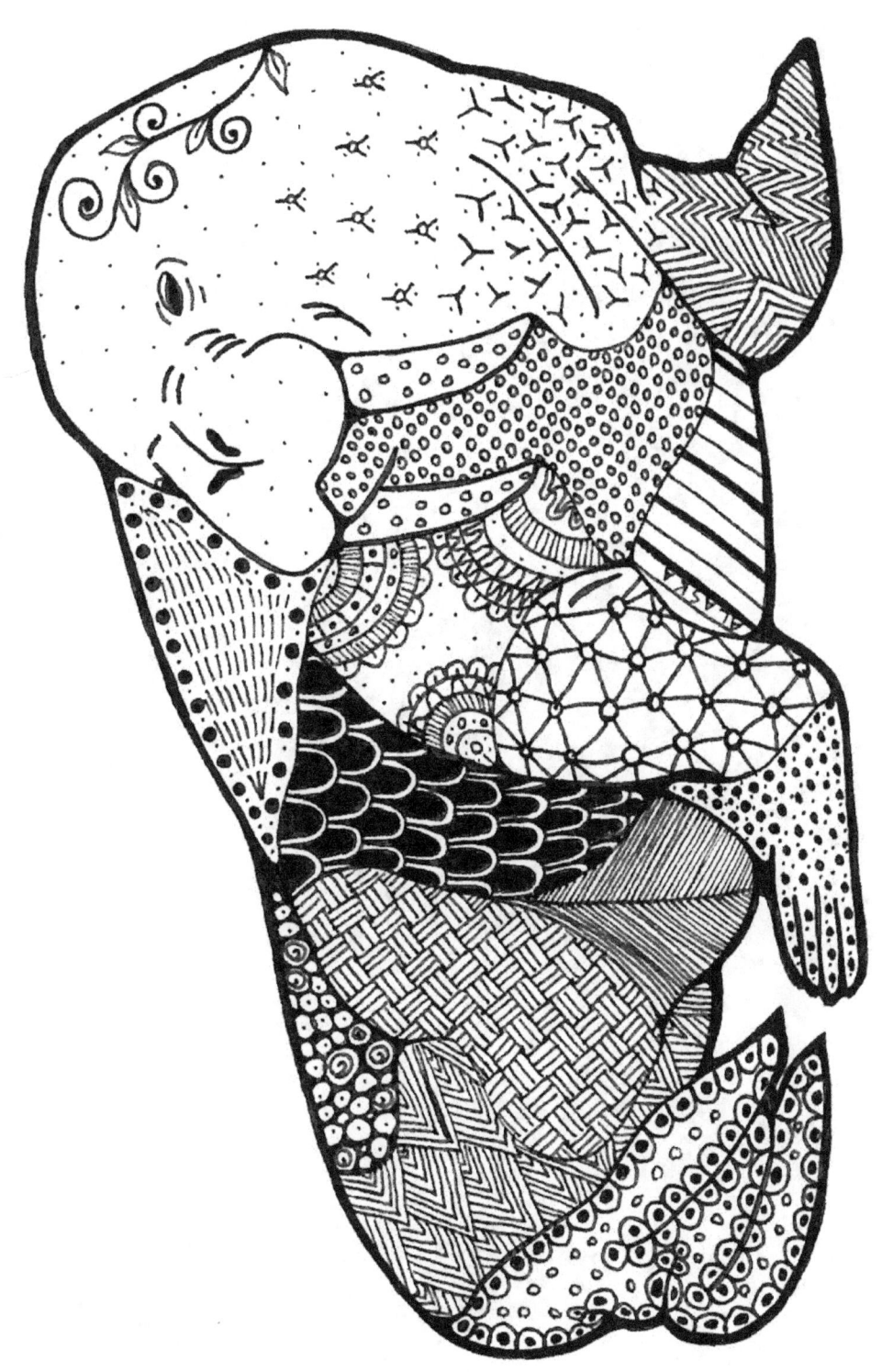

Pacific Walrus

Fun Fact: Their ivory tusks are upper canines that keep growing throughout their life.

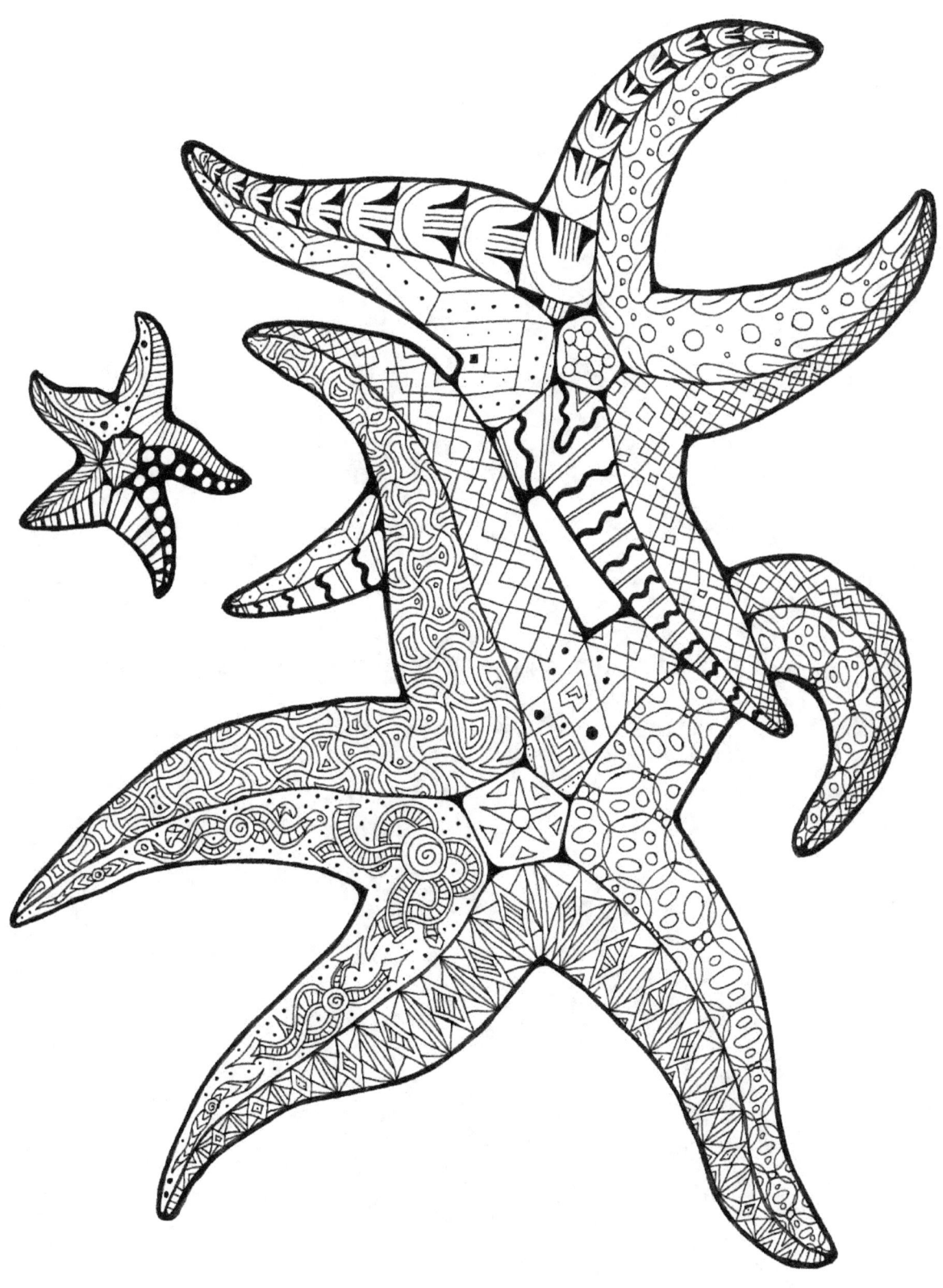

Starfish

Fun Fact: Most starfish travel at a rate of inches per hour.

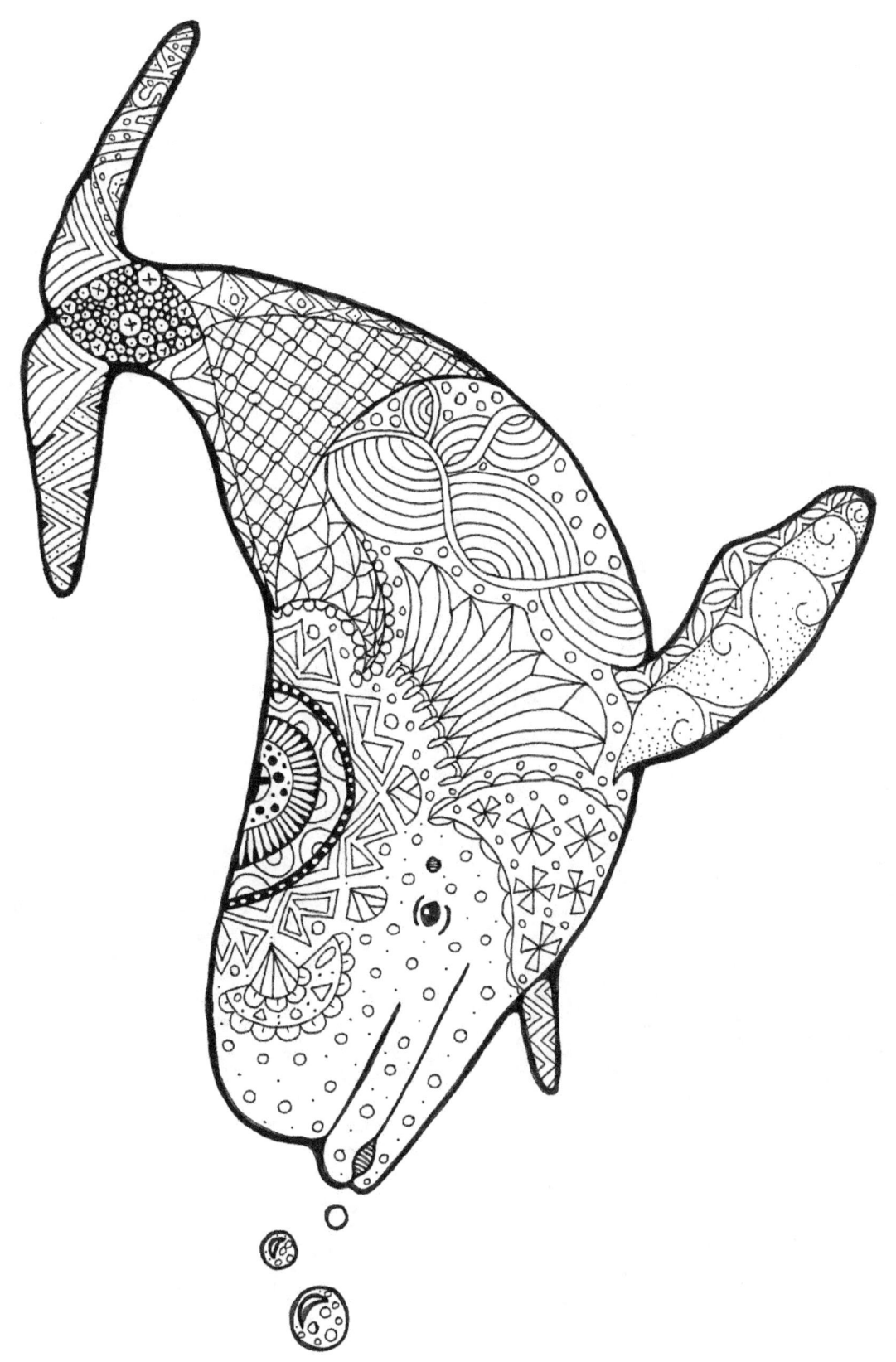

Beluga Whale

Fun Fact: These whales are born gray and turn white as they grow older. There are 5 populations of belugas around Alaska.

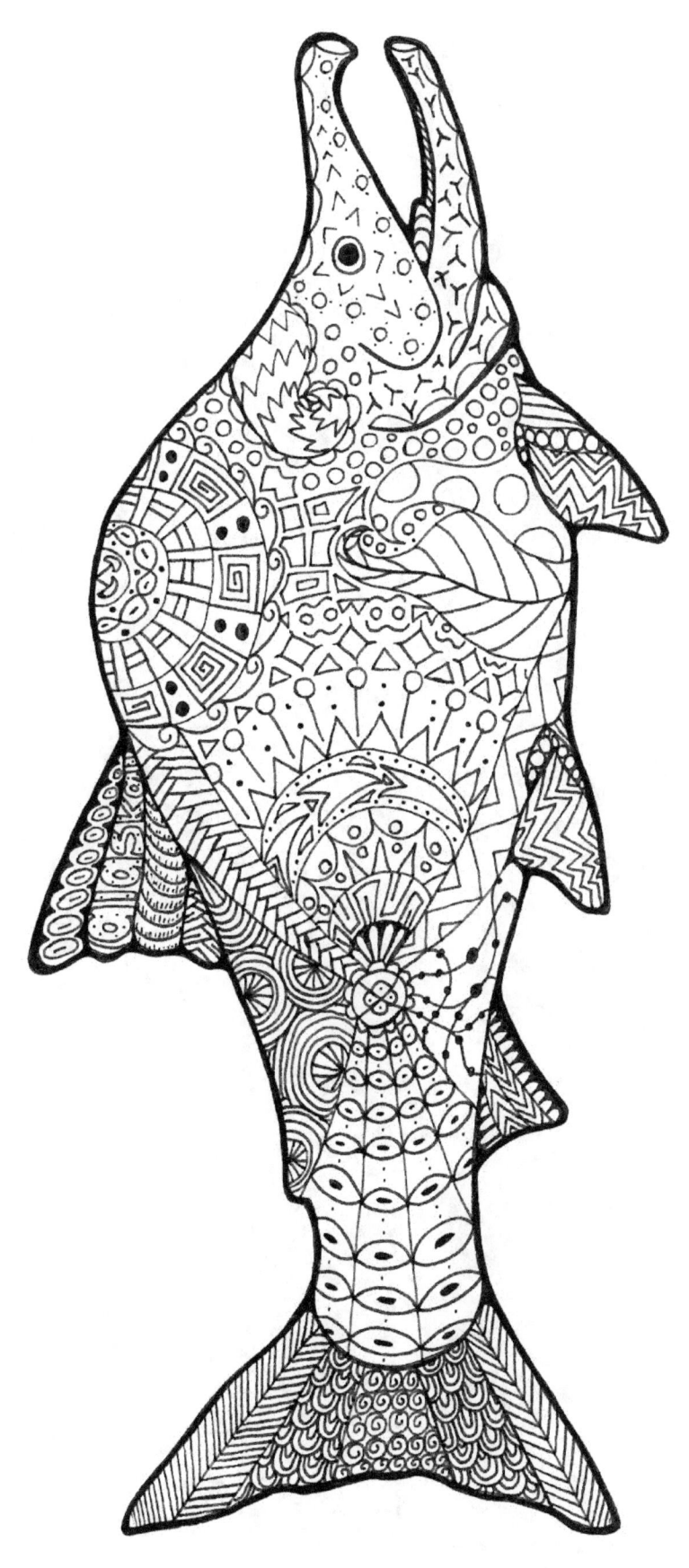

Sockeye Salmon

Fun Fact: When males reach breeding age they develop a hump and
their jaw becomes hooked.

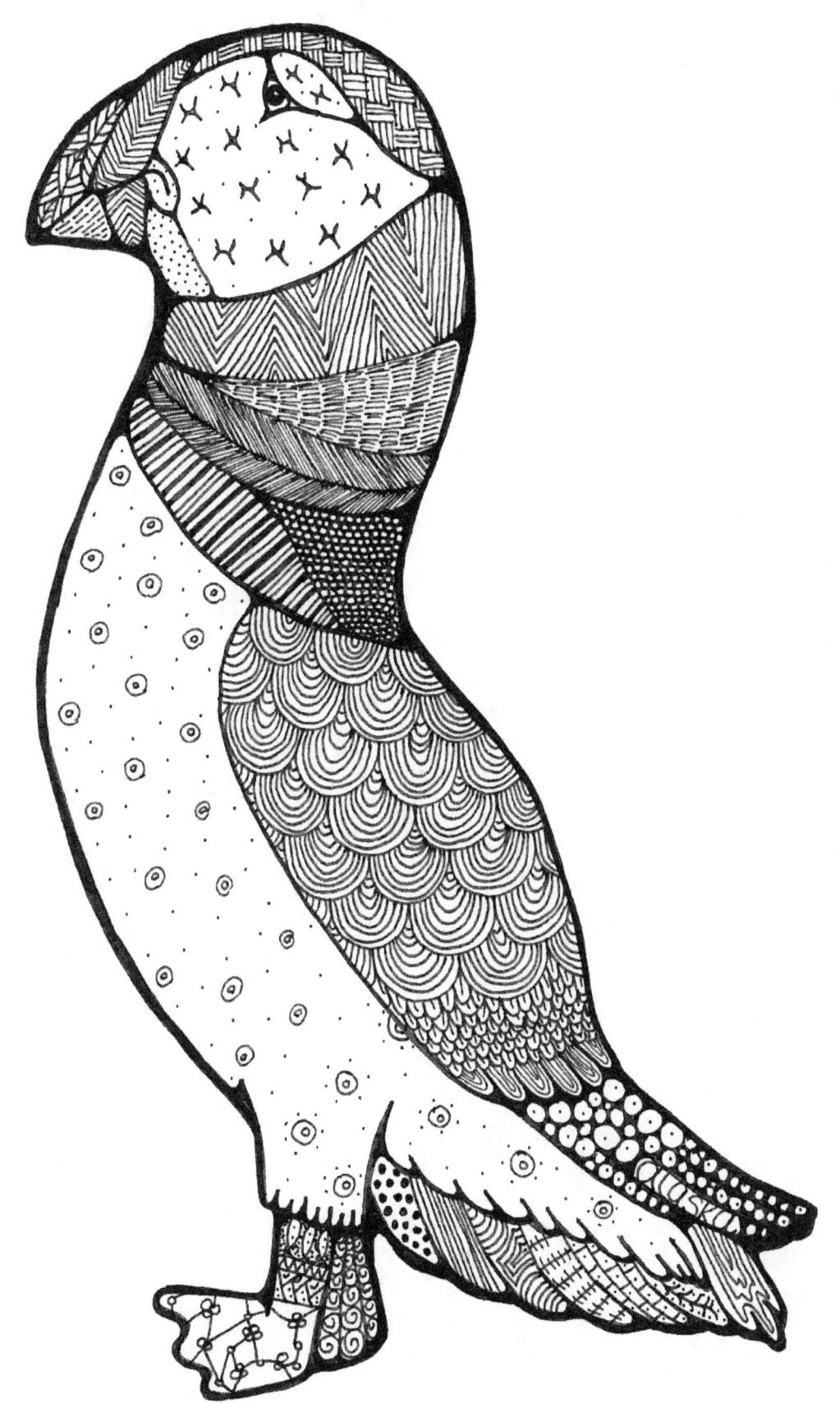

Horned Puffin

Fun Fact: Males and females have the same markings. These birds were dubbed "sea parrots" by early sailors.

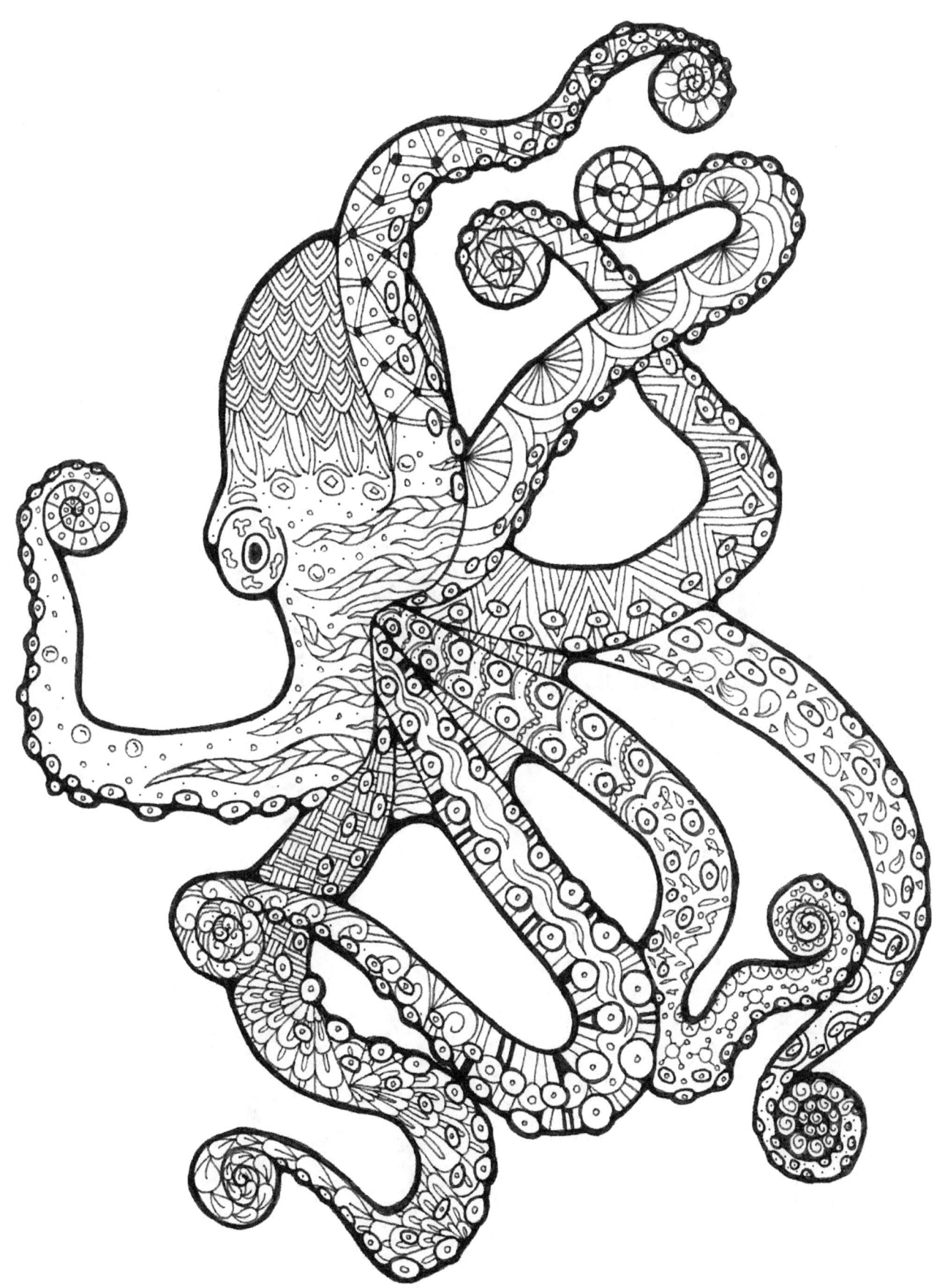

Giant Pacific Octopus

Fun Fact: These octopus have a short lifespan of only 3-5 years.
They are the largest species of octopus in the world.

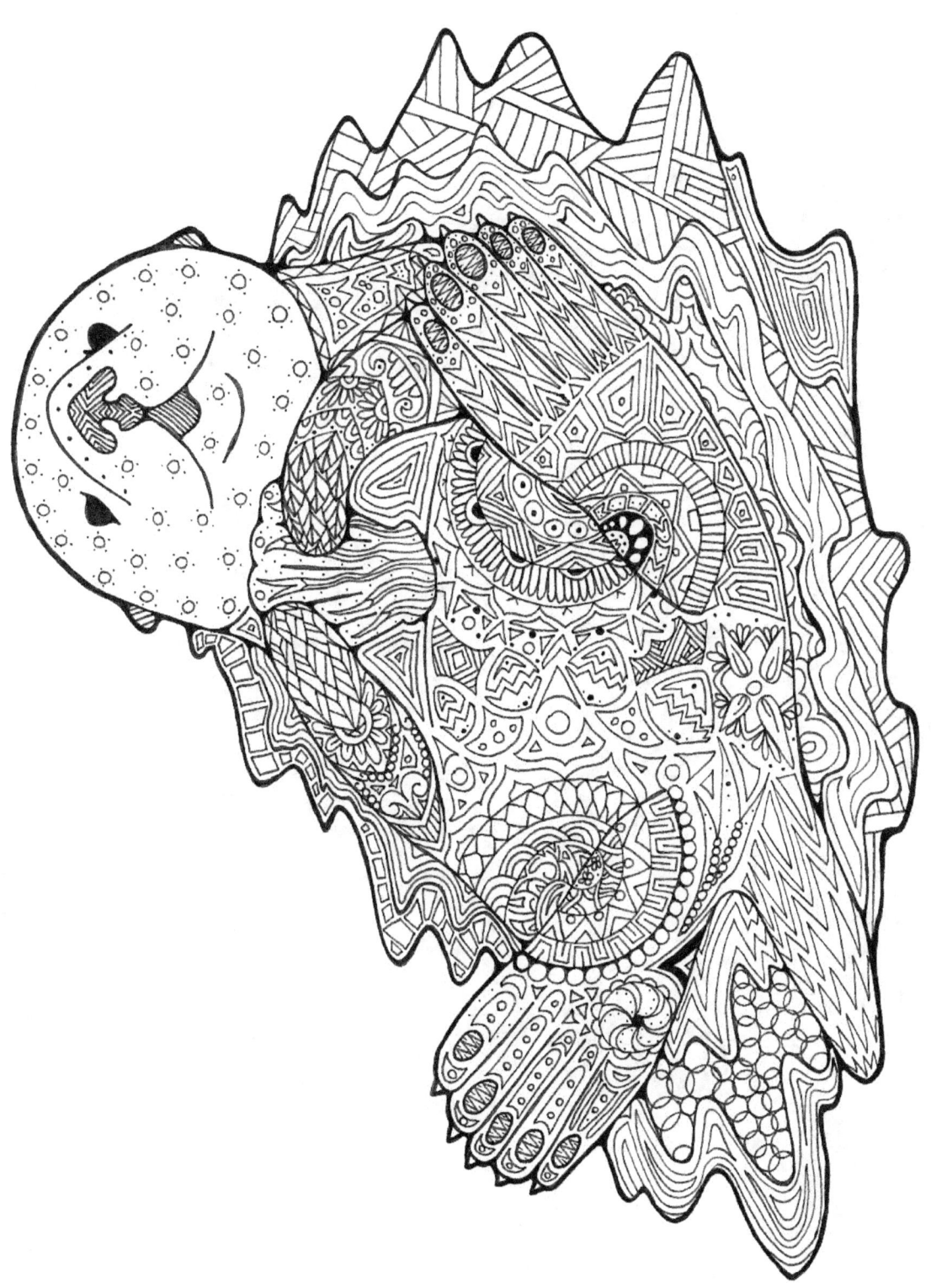

Northern Sea Otter

Fun Fact: Sea otters are the largest members of the weasel family.

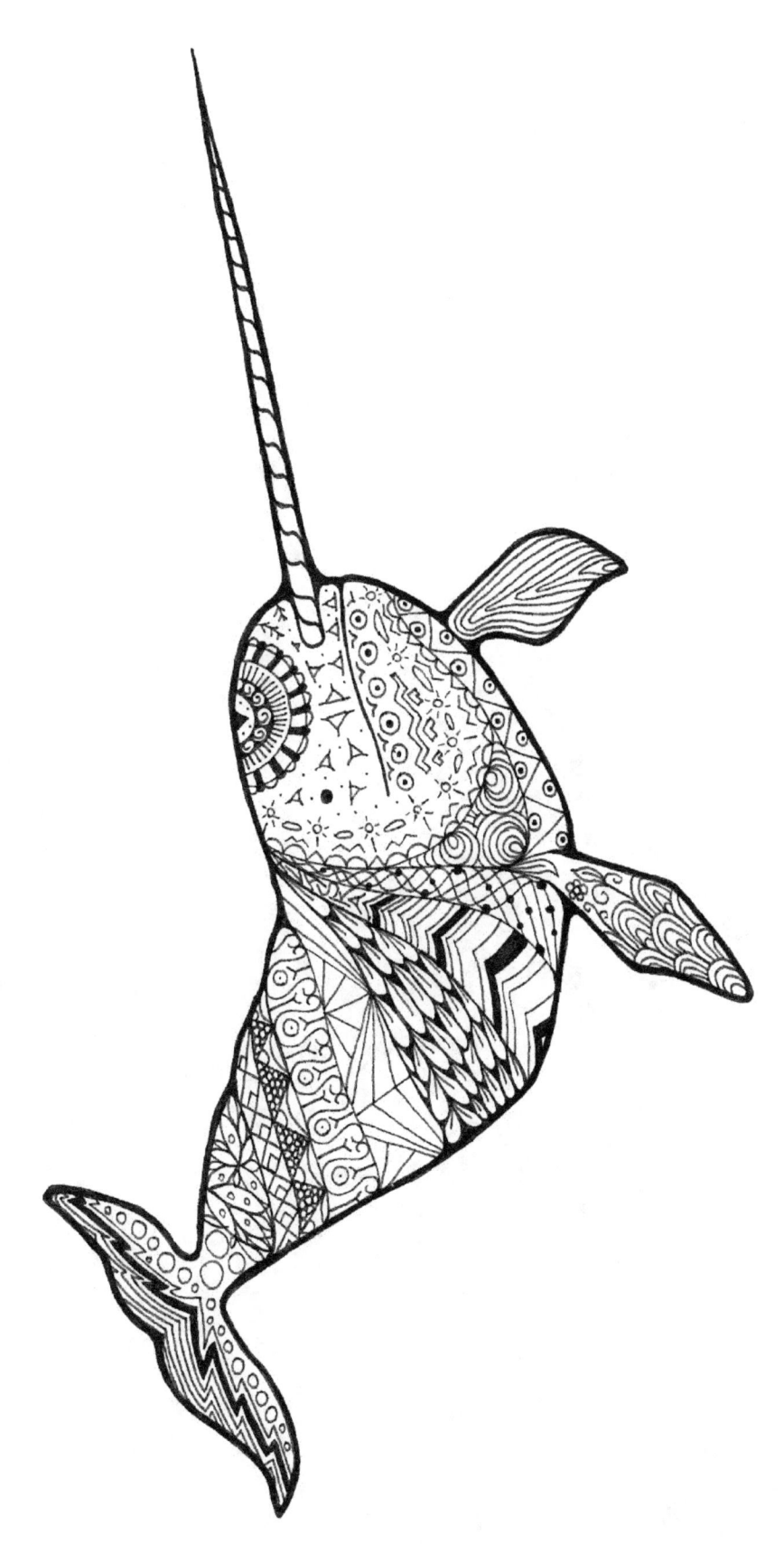

Narwhal (Narwhale)

Fun Fact: On males (and some females) the left of its two teeth can grow into a long ivory tusk jutting out from the front of the head. Narwhal and Beluga whales are very closely related.

About the Artist

Brittney is a former Army brat, turned Alaskan artist from Palmer (home to giant cabbage and the Alaska State Fair.) She lives with her much-loved pets and she loves living the Alaskan life. Brittney has always been the creative one in her family, crafting things since she was a child (she even has her 6th grade portfolio, full of wonderful works.) She began drawing her animals and other special projects about 2 years ago and found it very soothing. She hopes you find this coloring book as fun and relaxing as she does. To keep up with her future and present projects, like her page on Facebook: www.facebook.com/artbybrittneyk

If you are interested in a custom drawing or prices on art prints, please visit inkedfoxbybrittney.com or you may e-mail inkedfoxak@gmail.com

Finding Alaska Again: A Little Help

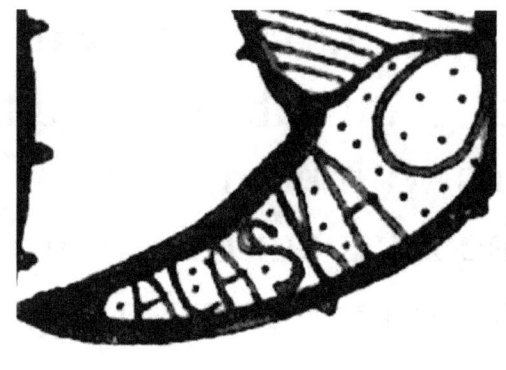

Red King Crab

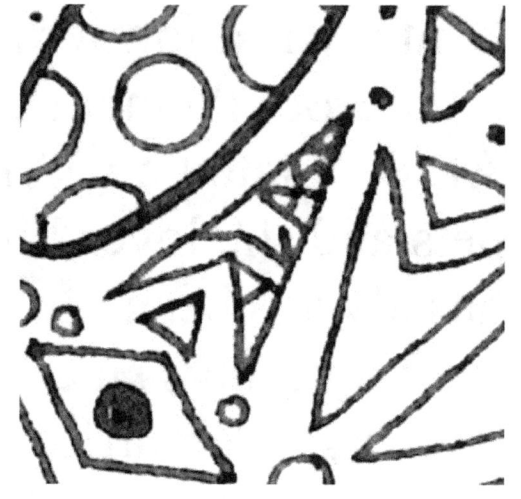

Jellyfish

Elephant Seal

Halibut

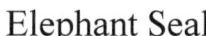

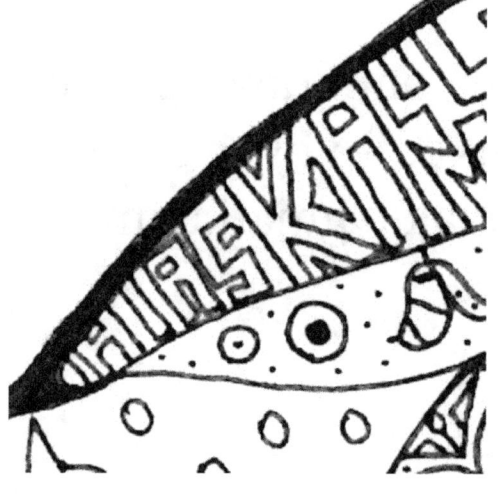

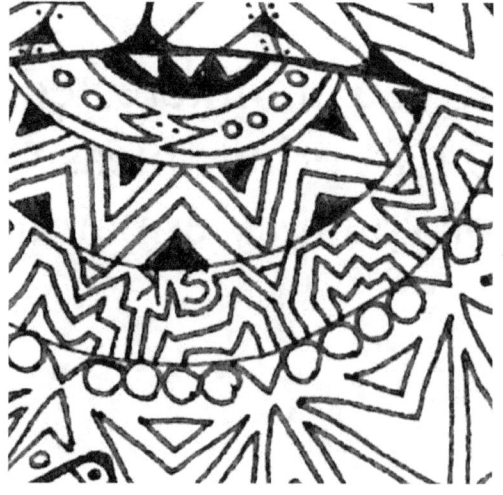

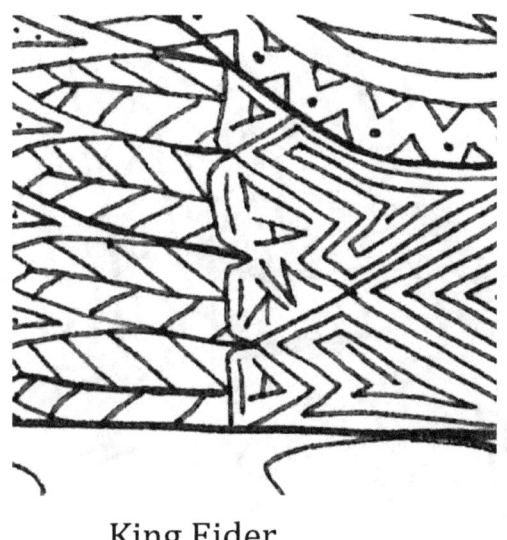

King Eider

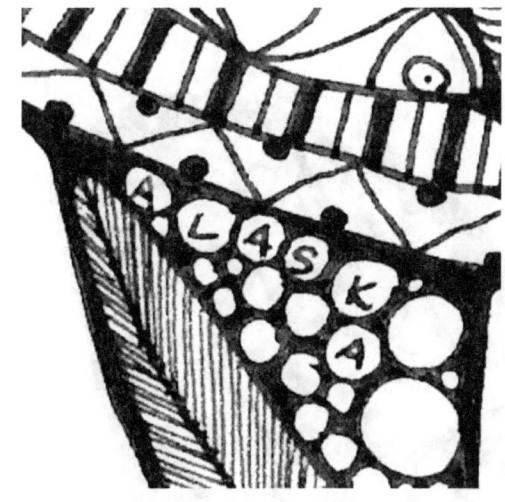

Humpback Whale

Steller Sea Lion

Pink Salmon

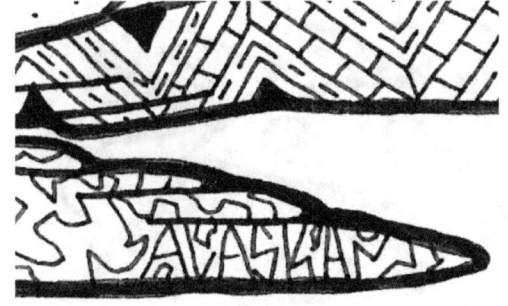

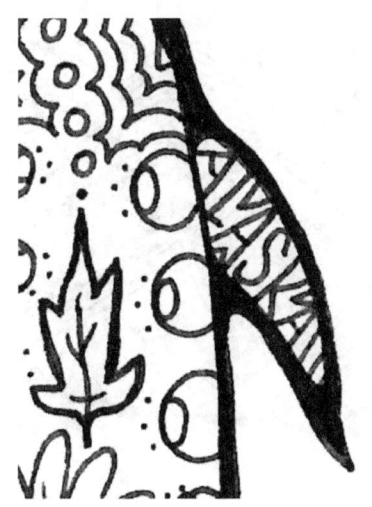

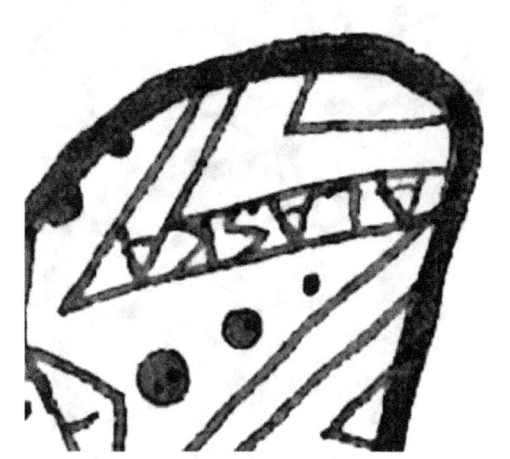

Leatherback Sea Turtle

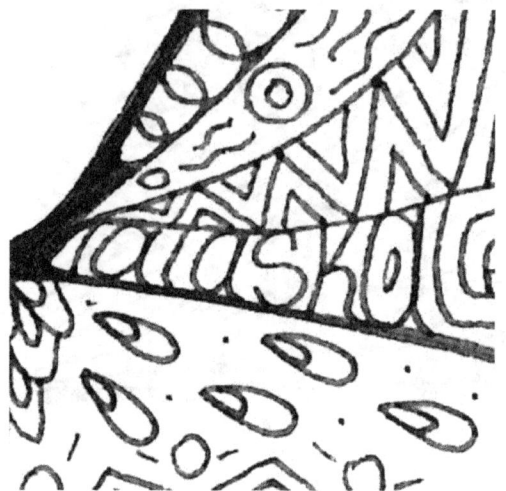

Salmon Shark

Harbor Seal

Orca

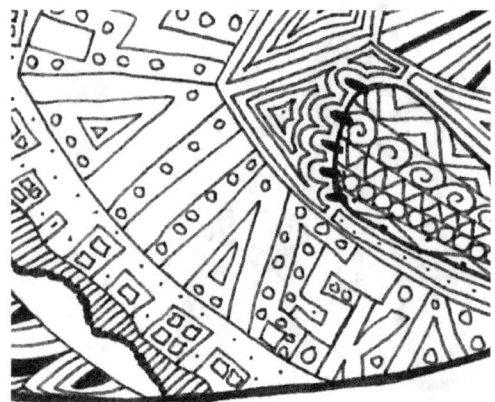

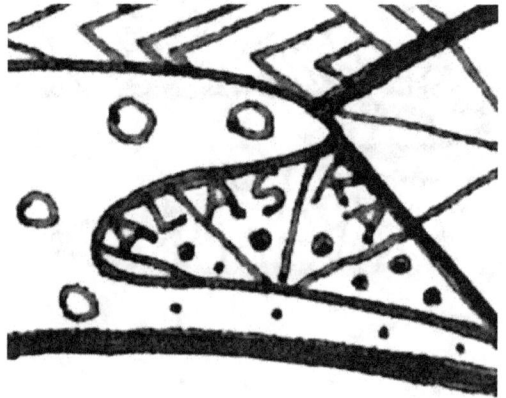

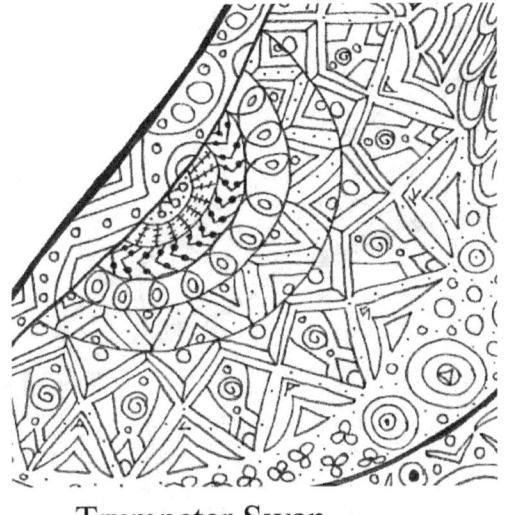

Trumpeter Swan

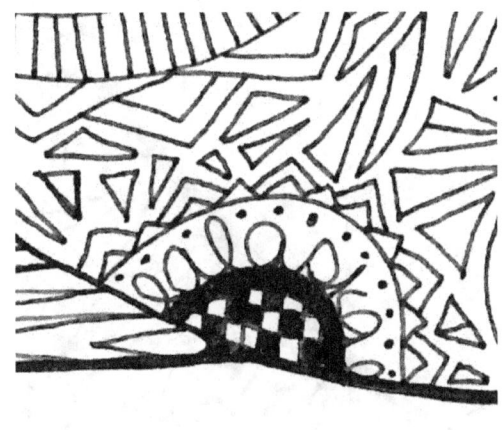

Beaver

Wood Frog

Walrus

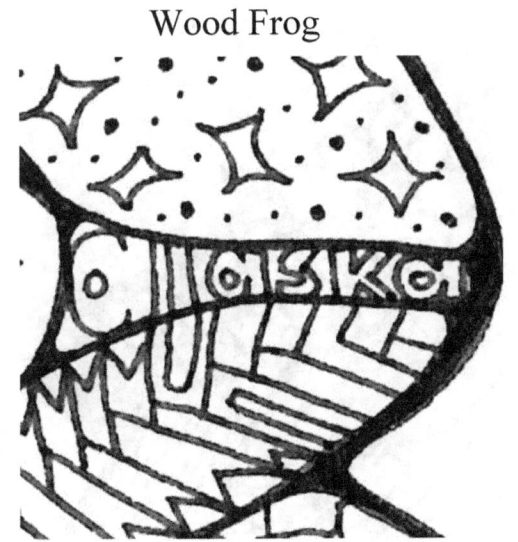

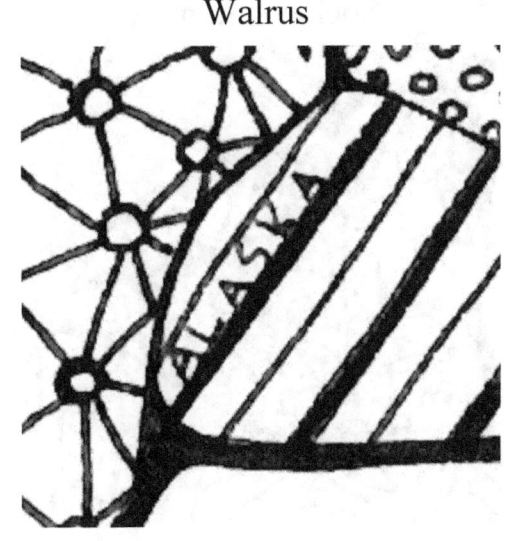

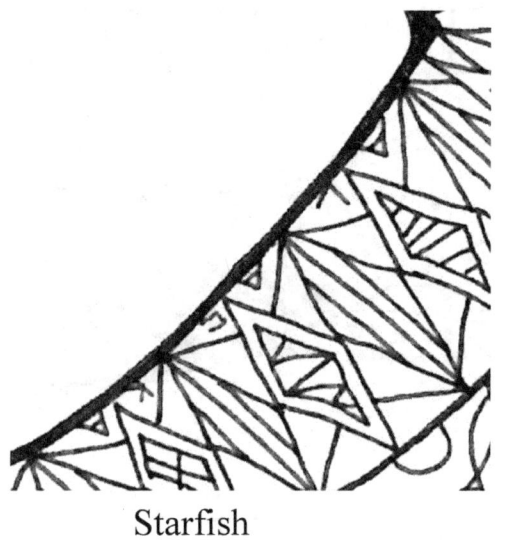

Starfish

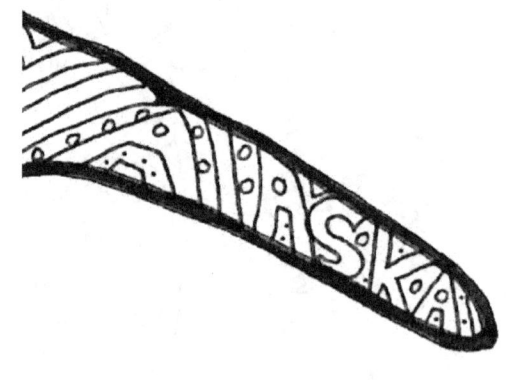

Beluga Whale

Sockeye Salmon

Horned Puffin

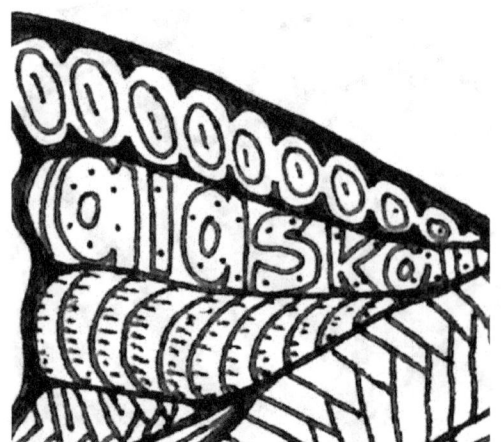

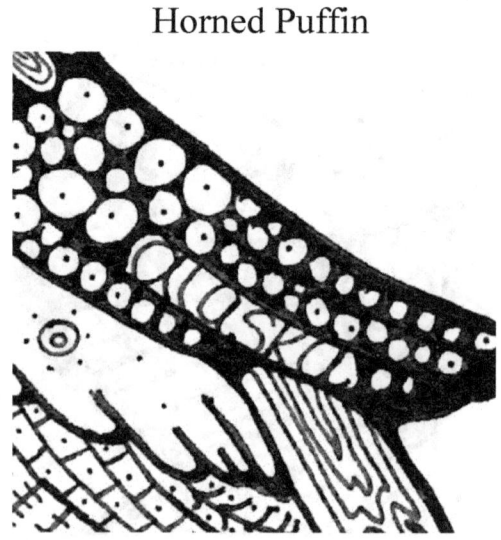

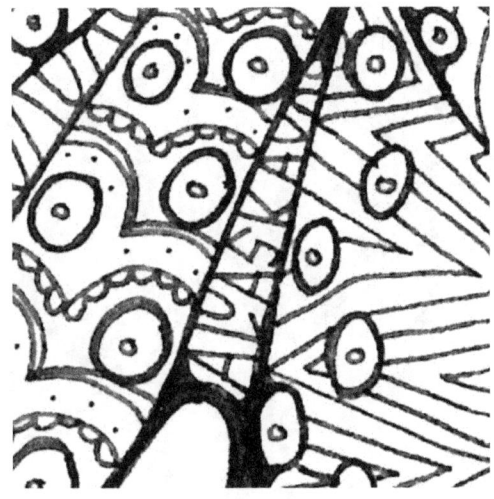

Giant Pacific Octopus

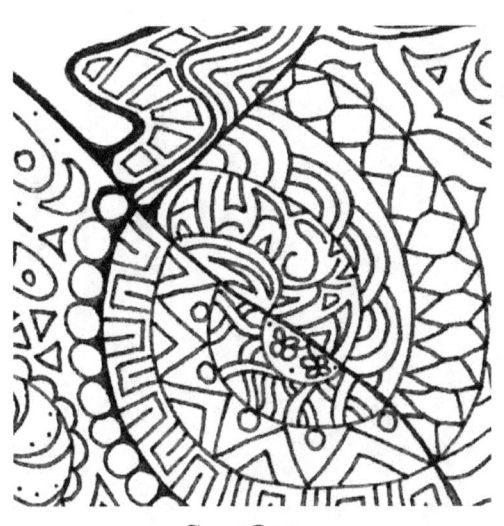

Sea Otter

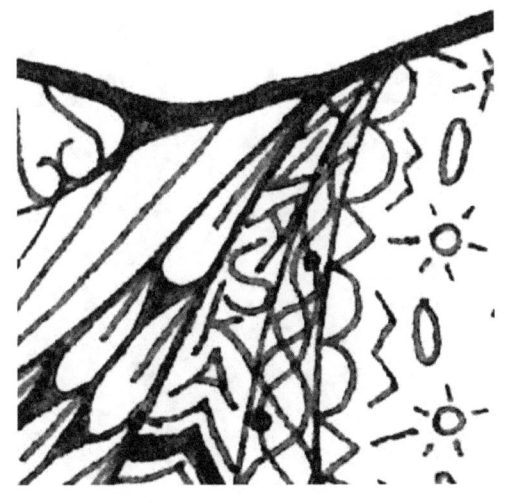

Narwhal

www.ingramcontent.com/pod-product-compliance
Lightning Source LLC
Chambersburg PA
CBHW080839170526
45158CB00009B/2587

9780692515112